Zero Inbox Changes Everything

How many emails do you have in your inbox right now? Hundreds? Thousands? Less than 50?

It's a bit of a misleading question, as an "appropriate" answer will vary depending on how many emails you typically receive each day. My Dad, for example, has worked outdoors for much of his life and is relatively new to his office-based job. He doesn't get many emails and, since he's still learning his way around the computer, the emails he does receive tend to take him a long time to reply to. Receiving 15 emails in a day is a big deal for my Dad.

I receive about 200 emails per day. And many people receive significantly more per day. So the number of emails in your inbox is probably not the right metric to focus on when talking about email productivity.

So instead: when was the last time you had an empty inbox? How *often* do you have no emails at all in your inbox?

We're getting closer. But we still haven't arrived at a complete picture, because I've learned that many people like to "file" their emails away. They create folders in Outlook or Gmail and dutifully file all new emails away as soon as they hear the familiar *ping* of an email alert, feeling very productive and clever. They have a folder for Personal emails, a folder for Newsletters, a folder for Client emails and a folder for Jokes and Things To Read. They may even have a folder for notes and reminders that they've emailed to themselves.

Here's your first lesson:

Filing emails does not work.

There is never a good reason to move an email *that has not been actioned* out of the inbox. Just because you've moved an email out of your inbox does not mean that you have gone any way towards your goal of taming your inbox. Moving emails around into various folders and filing systems is pointless busywork that may make you *feel* productive at the time, but in fact only creates extra work for yourself. It creates a cloud of obligation and responsibility over your head as you simply move emails around, always promising yourself that you'll deal with them "later".

Let's face it: later never comes. Have you ever actually gone through these email storage folders and completely cleared them? Or have more emails accumulated in the folders before you could completely process the older ones?

So an empty inbox with bulging email storage folders is not the right metric to focus on either.

No, I'm talking about true Zero Inbox.

True Zero Inbox is where all emails have been *actioned*. An email is actioned when there is nothing left to do on it.

- If it's rubbish, it's been deleted.
- If it was a quick FYI, you've noted whatever it contained and have sent an equally quick acknowledgement reply.
- If it contained an appointment, you've RSVP'd and noted the appointment in your calendar.
- If it contained a 100-page form that needed to be printed, completed by hand, scanned, and sent back (presumably to someone from 1997), you've done it.
- If it was a joke, you've read it (and forwarded it on, if that's your thing).

That is true Zero Inbox – when there is nothing left to do.

So when was the last time you achieved Zero Inbox? And how often do you achieve Zero Inbox?

Unless your answers were "today" and "every day" respectively, you've got work to do.

And I can promise you this: follow the simple rules in this book and you will get to the point where you *will* achieve Zero Inbox.

Every. Single. Day.

Call me weird, but there is no greater sense of achievement – no, *relief* – than knowing your emails are completely up to date.

Zero Inbox changes *everything*.

Step 1 – Understanding Why Zero Inbox Is So Important

The Death of Your Cluttered Inbox – Working Through The 7 Stages of Grief

You've been living with your cluttered inbox for a long time now, probably more than a decade. The fact is that when emails were first introduced into everyday life, no one ever taught us how to deal with them. Like most aspects of modern technology and social media, emails began as little more than a technological experiment and no one could ever truly predict whether it would be a passing fad or something that was here to stay.

Email evolved and increased steadily over time, and for most of us we can clearly remember those days when receiving an email was a momentous occasion in your life (after all, you had to tie up the phone line in order to connect to your expensive dial-up Internet connection just to see if there was a new email in the first place).

From that point onwards, emails became less of an obscure treat and more of a necessity of life. No longer do people ask: *Do you have email?* Instead, today the question is more along the lines of: *What's your email address?* Or simply: *Text me your email.*

Not only do we no longer have to tie up our home phone line in order to check our emails once or twice a day, we are now bombarded with an ongoing flurry of email activity every waking moment. The majority of people access their emails via a mobile device, and even if you have resisted this final frontier of the email invasion into our lives, you can guarantee that the steady stream of emails confronts you every time you are seated at your computer.

My point is that no one ever really decided to "start using email." For those of us older than 30, email was tentatively introduced into our lives sometime in the last 15-20 years, and became more necessary as society embraced the new technology. For younger people, email became a part of your lives from a young age, and its importance and level of necessity only increased as you made your way through school, further education, and into your working lives.

If you are like most people, email presents a constant form of stress. This stress of emails you haven't yet answered; the worry of emails being added to your ever-growing inbox after you hadn't *quite* finished tackling the emails from yesterday; and the anxiety caused by wondering if you've somehow missed an important email along the way.

In this book, I will show you how to whittle your email inbox down to zero (the elusive *Zero Inbox*) and how to keep it that way forever. For most people, this sounds like an unattainable yet highly desirable dream: imagine always being on top of your inbox! Yet at the same time, you'll be losing something: your cluttered inbox. While never having to deal with a cluttered inbox ever again is, of course, a wonderful thing, you will still to some extent go through the same process that you would if you "lost" anything else.

So here I present the seven stages of grief as they apply to what will very soon be the death of your cluttered inbox.

Stage 1: Shock & Denial

You're probably starting out wondering something along the lines of: *So what's the big deal? Why all the fuss?*

Most people deny that they have a problem with their emails. People are happy to joke about how "behind" that are with their emails, or even brag about how overflowing their inbox is when they compete with other people to see who is busier. An overstuffed inbox has become a bragging right, the calling card of a perpetually busy and important person.

You might even be shocked that I'm suggesting that your cluttered inbox causes stress at work, stress at home, difficulties sleeping, lack of productivity, reduced professional image, and even poor job performance.

You may also be thinking that you've been coping just fine with the daily email onslaught without adding new rules and procedures to your already busy day. After all, you barely have time to deal with the emails that you do manage to reply to, without spending even more time in your inbox.

In this stage, you're questioning whether this book even has any relevance to you.

Let's just accept that as a given, and move on to Stage 2.

Stage 2: Pain & Guilt

Let me ask you a question. Have you ever dreaded opening your inbox in the morning because you were afraid that there would be a "friendly reminder" from someone – perhaps a co-worker, family member, client, or your boss – whose original email still sat there unanswered in your inbox, or worse, filed away?

I ask because I know the feeling myself. I know it all too well. Sometimes I've even caught myself squinting my eyes as Outlook opened, to check if it was safe. Reading one of the earlier drafts of this book, my Mum admitted that sometimes she pretends she can't see the subject lines of her emails because she doesn't want to know what's there.

Emails can bring such a mixed bag of emotions: funny jokes and trivialities to lighten your mood and give you something to procrastinate with; loving, happy or friendly emails from family or friends; or, at the other end of the spectrum: angry and impatient emails from people who are waiting for you to do something.

The stress and anxiety that comes from dreading the state of your inbox is a very real source of pain. While people often joke about emails and the size of the inboxes, the pain I'm referring to here is no laughing matter. It's the type of pain that fills you with dread and, at times, makes you avoid your inbox altogether, or may even cause you to take a day off work or to otherwise procrastinate.

So that's pain, as for guilt: what else would you call that feeling when you know you should have done something, but you haven't managed to carve out the time just yet? Perhaps someone emailed you some forms over a week ago and, although you know that filling them out and emailing them back would be a relatively straightforward task, that email is sitting there competing with the hundreds of other emails waiting your attention, and you just haven't got around to it yet. Or perhaps someone sent you an email that you genuinely didn't see, because your inbox was so overflowing that it slipped your notice.

That feeling when you run into a colleague or a friend and you *know* you're both thinking about whatever it was they emailed you about over a week ago that you haven't replied to yet – whether it was a personal email or something work-related – is nothing short of guilt.

We've established that a cluttered inbox can undoubtedly (and quite often) be a very real source of pain and guilt, so let's move on to Stage 3.

Stage 3: Anger & Bargaining

Why does email have to infect every facet of our lives? Why is it that we can't even sit down for a meal or spend some quality time with our family or friends without being constantly notified of new messages? Society didn't crumble and the workforce didn't grind to a halt two decades ago when email didn't even exist, so why has it become such a necessity today?

These are all important and valid questions, and you, like many people, have every right to demand answers to these hypothetical questions. Email has become little more than a constant interruption in our otherwise enjoyable lives. You're not the only person to feel a sense of anger and almost a sense that you have been violated by the constant intrusion of emails into your life.

As for bargaining: have you ever considered having someone else take care of your emails? Perhaps you have an assistant with access to your inbox, or perhaps you've even tried having an online freelancer help you to manage the day-to-day responsibility.

Or perhaps you've tried to walk away from your emails: turning your computer and mobile devices off so the emails couldn't reach you. But what happened when you inevitably returned? All the old emails, plus a bunch of new ones, were waiting for you.

Emails are essentially a personal form of communication, and ultimately the responsibility to manage your inbox falls back on you. Hiring someone to help you delete unwanted newsletters, or dictating your email replies for someone else to type and send on your behalf is not the most efficient and effective way of dealing with email.

But you wouldn't be the first person to try to bargain your way out of your inbox.

Stage 4: Depression, Reflection, Loneliness

As much as we'd like to oscillate between ignoring our inboxes, lamenting over the speed at which the problem is growing, and joking about the unmanageable burden with others, the fact is that you are eventually going to have to deal with every single one of those emails currently sitting in your inbox. Even if the way you "deal" with it is simply to delete it and pretend you never saw it in the first place (I've been there, too), you're still going to take some kind of action on that email at some stage.

Maybe you're going to delete it, maybe you're going to forward it to someone else to deal with, maybe you need to send a quick confirmation reply and add something to your calendar, or maybe it will require a comprehensive reply that will take you several hours to prepare. Whatever that looks like for you, one thing is certain: you're going to have to do it eventually.

Here's one more thing to consider. While you're busy procrastinating and putting off replying to the emails that are currently in your inbox, more emails are flooding in. You're well-aware that the stream of emails is more or less constant, even overnight.

If you don't make the effort to keep up-to-date with your inbox, emails will take over your life, and I'm not being melodramatic. If you've ever had trouble falling asleep or experienced difficulty relaxing and winding down in your own time because you were preoccupied by thoughts of something in your inbox, then you know that what I'm saying is true. When not properly managed, emails can and will take over your life.

If that doesn't summon depression, reflection, and loneliness: what does?

Stage 5: The Upward Turn

Finally, we start to see the first ray of sunshine that hints of the end of the tunnel.

We've established that you will eventually have two take action on every single email in your inbox, even if that just means doing what many of us have thought about while lying awake at 2am: pressing Ctrl+A (select all), closing your eyes, and then pressing Delete. Whether it happens now, next week, or in a year from now, one thing is clear: those emails can't stay there forever.

Here's a question: given that the above is true, what would your life be like if you simply took that action *now*, rather than putting it off until some unforeseeable time in the future?

Either way, you still have to spend the time and energy dealing with that email in whatever way you're going to. It has to happen sometime, so instead of spending hours scrolling through, scheduling, sorting, and filing your emails, what if you just replied... Now?

Stage 6: Reconstruction & Working Through

Now we're getting somewhere. Let's keep powering through.

Here's what will change in your life (there is little doubt that dealing with your inbox is part of life itself, as there are very few aspects of life that don't involve email in some way – work, family, holidays, finances, dreams and aspirations – nothing is immune) if you decide to action your emails now rather than later:

- You will have a sense of achievement from having completed a task in good time, compared to that strange sense that doesn't seem to have a name where you complete a task late. It's definitely not a feeling of accomplishment, it's like a mixture of three parts guilt and one part relief.
- Replies and follow-ups to your emails will be of the happy, thankful variety, compared to the terse nudges full of complaints.
- You could even look forward to opening your inbox each morning, compared to the sense of dread and foreboding (possibly including eye-squinting) that you have experienced in the past.
- You will actually be doing your job, rather than putting off the tasks you are likely being paid to complete either until the very last second or until the other party is complaining so loudly and frequently that you just can't ignore them any longer.

Given that the workload is exactly the same – again, you will have to action those emails at some stage – are there any possible advantages of not taking that action now?

Stage 7: Acceptance & Hope

Are you starting to see the light at the end of the tunnel? I can show you how to completely deal with your backlog of emails, no matter how overwhelming it may seem right now, so that your inbox is completely empty and every email has been actioned. I will then show you how to deal with your emails on an ongoing basis so that you can achieve Zero Inbox every day.

None of it is difficult, and it's not going to cost you anything. What it does take, though, is a change of mindset and a willingness to let go of your email struggles (which, for too many people, can be akin to the calling card of a busy and important person) and to actually *want* to be free of the stress and worry associated with an out-of-control inbox.

All I need is your cooperation, and I guarantee you can make it happen.

Here are my promises to you (and I don't take these promises lightly):

- Zero Inbox will make your work and life easier.
- Zero Inbox will reduce your stress levels.
- Zero Inbox will make your current customers/colleagues like you (and will bring in new customers).
- Zero Inbox will move you along the scale towards actually enjoying your job.
- Zero Inbox will stop you from dreading checking your emails.
- Zero Inbox will make you appear more of a leader and less of a follower.

I can also promise you that there is nothing else you need to buy. I'm not selling a program or a course or software or an app. Heck, right now I don't even have a website. Everything you need is contained within this book. Just follow the steps as I have laid them out in this book and your life will change.

Step 2 – Work Through The Backlog

Filling the Void

I mentioned above that you, like the vast majority of people, have been living with your cluttered inbox for years, if not decades. I went through the seven stages of grief because, in a very real way, forever eliminating your cluttered inbox and having your emails being manageable on a daily basis involves you saying goodbye to something that has been a part of your life for so long.

Many people, myself included, have a fear of having nothing to do. For me, it is comforting to have a long to-do list: one that I know I will never fully get through. As much as I outwardly proclaim that my aim is to one day finish my to-do list, in reality I would be terrified to do so.

From speaking with other people, I've found that this is a very common occurrence, especially with people who are self-employed. We've come to equate being busy with making money, as well as the *appearance* of being busy with the *appearance* of being successful.

For other people, a full to-do list gives them a legitimate way to procrastinate from harder, more substantive business tasks. Somehow, not completing your tax return or writing your annual business forecast because you're dreadfully busy sorting through thousands of unactioned emails just doesn't *seem* like procrastinating, whereas avoiding the tax return or business forecast by scrolling through Facebook or playing Candy Crush undoubtedly is.

You may well have a different psychological basis for this fear, but for the purpose of this book, you simply need to understand that there is a part of you that is holding on very tightly to your cluttered inbox, and the massive "to do" that goes along with it. For this reason, you will very likely find that you try to sabotage yourself in your initial quest to reach Zero Inbox.

Working through your email backlog is going to be a mammoth task, and the daily maintenance your inbox will require in future will pale in comparison to the task you're getting ready to tackle right now. From the point of view of your subconscious mind, this is the perfect time to put the whole endeavour into the too hard basket and to find another simpler task that will provide a sense of immediate satisfaction.

But here's the good news. Simply *being aware* of this phenomenon can be all that takes to overcome it. When you feel yourself pulling away from the project – especially during this backlog stage – simply recognise and understand that it is your subconscious mind trying to thwart your attempts to free up your time in the future and to remove your cluttered inbox from your list of ongoing time-consuming tasks.

In addition, many people equate a full inbox with being terribly busy and important. We tie up our ego in our email inbox, convinced that the more emails we receive each day, the more important we surely must be.

Thinking about this rationally, the logic of this argument is surely flawed. Anyone can accumulate hundreds or even thousands of emails, but it is only an organised, professional, and efficient person who can keep their inbox under control. So instead of thinking about your 3,000 unread emails as a bragging right, change your mindset and think about it as a time management failing on your part. Critically, keep this mindset when listening to other people boast about how many emails they receive on a daily basis and how full their inbox currently is.

Turn the topic on its head and know that the *less* cluttered your inbox is, the more busy and important you surely are. You are busy because it takes time to achieve Zero Inbox every day, and by doing so you know you are spending your valuable time wisely by staying on top of your commitments and replying in a timely manner to your important correspondence. And you are important because, well, no one can be *that* important if it doesn't matter if emails remain unanswered for months, or are ignored altogether.

The advice here is just to be aware that you may try to sabotage yourself during this process, because part of your ego is tied up in your overstuffed ego. Simply recognise this resistance for what it is and push through. Once you've worked through the backlog and achieved Zero Inbox – potentially for the first time ever – you'll notice your mindset begin to change.

How to Search Your Archives

Before we begin the process of working through your email backlog, let's take a moment to take care of the storage folders within your inbox. I say *folders* as a plural because most people seem to think that they need multiple folders in which to store their saved emails. By *saved emails* I'm referring to emails that have successfully been actioned.

You may think that I would advise you to delete an email once it has been fully actioned, but on the contrary, I believe emails should properly be stored in case they are needed in the future. And with storage not being a problem these days – unlike only a few years ago, when data storage was a major issue – it will barely make a difference to your overall storage levels or the speed of your computer if you choose to keep most important emails just in case you need them in the future. You'll be glad you did in the event that you ever need to refer back to them, or if proof of having sent or received an email is ever needed, for example in a legal matter.

I'll admit that it wasn't long ago that multiple storage folders were a necessity. Search bars within major email clients are a relatively new addition, giving you the ability to search through all items within your email program to find the emails that meets your specific search criteria. Prior to this, you were in the position of having to scroll through previous emails to find the one that you are looking for, so it did make sense to create various storage folders and file your emails accordingly. For example, if you needed to locate an email sent a week ago regarding a specific project, it would be much more efficient to scroll through emails contained within a folder related solely to that project, rather than scrolling past personal emails and other unrelated work email in order to find what you were looking for.

These days, though, the landscape has changed dramatically and searching through your entire email archives is as simple as entering the appropriate search criteria, directing your email client to look through all folders, and waiting for the right result to come up.

For this reason, you only need to have *one* storage folder to put all your actioned emails. Personally, I call this folder *Actioned Emails* (strangely enough) and I am fairly indiscriminate when I put emails in there to live. Obviously if an email is pure junk and can properly be deleted, that's the course of action that should be taken. But if it's anything that I have replied to or even read in any detail, I'll dispose of that are putting it in my Actioned Emails folder.

I also periodically empty my sent items directly into my Actioned Emails folder. If I have sent an email then I want to keep a record of it, just in case it is ever needed in the future. Emails can easily be tampered with or forged, so you are wise to keep spotless records of every email you send.

Name your one storage folder whatever you'd like, but I would avoid including the word Archive in the name of the folder. Email archiving is a completely separate matter and not one that should be confused with your own personal storage folder for keeping all actioned and sent items.

Before we begin working through the backlog in your inbox, start by creating your personal Actioned Emails folder, or whatever else you choose to call it, within the structure of your inbox. Now, start dumping the contents of any other storage folder into it.

For now, leave your inbox alone, but if you already have *previously actioned* emails stored in other storage folders (and I'm guessing you do: it seems highly unlikely that your inbox would be a mess but you'd have no other emails stored anywhere) then now is the time to empty those storage folders directly into your new Actioned Emails folder. To be clear: I am speaking only of old emails that you are completely finished with: there is nothing left to do with these emails, you are simply storing them for the sake of storing them.

Just trust that you will easily be able to find whatever you need with a simple search, and that you never need to scroll through the endless list of saved emails again.

Once you have emptied your previous folder structure into your new Actioned Emails folder, delete those old folders because you won't be using them again. Next, empty all of your sent items directly into your Actioned Emails folder.

By this stage you should have an inbox which is still full to bursting, an empty sent items folder, and a brand-new Actioned Emails folder that is starting to look pretty full.

If you have any other folders that contain emails, you need to sort them out before you go on to the next step. If the folders contain emails that you have *not actioned yet*, dump the contents directly into your inbox, ready for sorting in the next step. If the folders contain emails that you *have already actioned* and simply wished to keep a copy of: well, these should have been dumped into your Actioned Emails folder already. Do it now.

If you have folders that contain a mixture of old emails and emails that have yet to be actioned – for example, if you store all emails from a certain person in one folder, regardless of whether you have replied to the email yet or not – then for now dump the entire contents into your inbox so that you can sort it out properly later.

Done? Great, that's go on to the next step and start sorting through that backlog.

Working Through the Backlog

By this stage you've committed to taming your inbox and achieving Zero Inbox every day. Good for you! Chances are you are starting with a sizable amount of email backlog, otherwise you wouldn't be reading this book. The first thing you need to do is to work through that backlog. It is not going to be easy and it's not going to be quick, especially for those of you with tens of thousands or even hundreds of thousands of emails in the inbox. (Surely no one has more than a *million* emails, right?)

The silver lining is that this is a process you will only ever have to complete once, because after that you will be achieving Zero Inbox every day. You may potentially have to complete a smaller version of this task later if, for example, an email backlog builds up if you've taken an extended absence for a holiday or if you've been unwell. But rest assured that any future backlog tasks will pale in comparison to the task you're getting ready to complete right now.

This is a sizeable task you're about to undertake. You're going to be working through years of bad habits and poor email management, and you're going to spend a fair amount of time wading through your overstuffed inbox. But when you've finished you will to be presented with a thing of beauty: a completely and legitimately *empty inbox*. Not just one that appears empty but which has thousands of emails hidden away in folders, but one that actually *is* empty. Your inbox will be ready to receive tomorrow's emails, and you'll be ready to action new emails every day, never again having to apologise for a late reply.

Let's just concentrate on that for a second. I'm promising that you will never again have to begin an email with:

My apologies for the late reply.
Sorry for not getting back to you sooner.
Sorry to have kept you waiting.

Or whatever other you've typed out hundreds of times in the past.

Never again.

Things May Get Tough

Have you ever seen one of those decluttering shows, where someone like the Australian organising genius Peter Walsh will empty out the contents of someone's wardrobe and show them that they have 15 identical red button-up shirts? Or he'll try to find out why a family of six takes turns using the one downstairs shower even though the house has three large bathrooms, only to find that the other two bathrooms are completely packed to the ceiling with clothes, furniture, and boxes of junk?

Those shows seem frivolous and entertaining on the outside, but things can heat up and get emotional pretty fast. People are attached to their clutter, and what looks like a pile of rotting newspapers to one person can be another person's life achievement. It's the same with your inbox: you've been living this way for a long time, and it's not going to be easy to get rid of everything.

You're going to be arguing with yourself a lot, so just let the process happen. Recognise right now that, even though it seems silly and frivolous and even embarrassing, you are making a huge change here and, yes, you are going to be attached to some of the emails you've been saving, as well as the state of your inbox as a whole.

You are going to try to argue with yourself and with the advice given in this book.

Just be aware of this, and recognise the emotions as they come up. Try not to dismiss any thoughts or get annoyed with yourself for finding the process difficult at times. Just because we are working with bits of data on a computer does not make those emails any less real than physical clutter like clothes, shoes, DVDs, rotting newspapers or anything else that people keep.

The Aim of Working through Your Backlog

Once the backlog has been taking care of and you are faced with the daily mission of keeping your inbox under control, the aim will be to achieve Zero Inbox every day. At this stage, though, your aim while working through the backlog is not to achieve Zero Inbox.

Instead, the task is a lot easier: simply to become familiar with the contents of your inbox, to remove anything that has already been actioned or that requires no action, and to send off any quick replies that you can identify. At this stage, don't concern yourself with replying to complicated emails or doing anything that would take more than a couple of minutes of your time. Your emails have likely already been sitting there for some time, and right now an extra day isn't going to make any difference.

The Process of Clearing out Your Email Backlog

The first step in the process is to empty everything into one inbox. You will largely have completed this in the previous step, so this is just a reminder as to what the state of your emails should be at this stage.

If you have various email accounts, for example a personal email address as well as a business address, move the entire contents of one of your inboxes into the other. Don't worry, you can still reply from whichever email address you choose by when you do come to reply, regardless of where the email is currently stored.

If you have storage folders, meaning that you move emails from the inbox into folders to deal with later, move the entire contents of all of those folders into your inbox. Then delete the folders, because you will not be using them again.

If you have storage folders for emails that have already been actioned, you would already have moved these emails into your new Actioned Emails folder.

Now, let's tackle your inbox.

Arrange your inbox so that the emails are sorted by the From field. In Outlook, you will notice that at the top of your list of emails it will say "By Date" with an arrow pointing downwards. Click on "By Date" and change it to "Sort by Sender" and you will see that all the emails in your inbox are now sorted by the sender.

Why do we do this when clearing out your email backlog? Some of the emails in your backlog will have been sitting there waiting to be actioned for months, if not years. There is every chance that the same person has emailed you more than once, and it would be an exercise in futility for you to reply to the first chronological email from the person, only to find a subsequent email that may change the situation. For example, a colleague may have emailed you two weeks ago asking for some information, but then emailed again a week later to tell you not to bother. You will look very unprofessional if you action the first email, clearly not having read the second.

You have probably been receiving regular newsletters and updates from the same people over and over. Sorting by the From field means that you can make a decision about the whole batch of newsletters at once. If you decide to delete all 30 newsletters from your local grocery store (and you should) it would be a huge time saver to delete them all in one go than to make the same decision every time you come across one of newsletters while working in chronological order.

Read through each email from each new sender before replying. In some instances, it may be appropriate to send one reply – a compilation email – to cover the questions raised within all of the emails sent from that person. In other instances, it will be more appropriate for you to reply to each individual email separately. It all depends on whether the sender has deliberately focused on separate subjects in each email. It should be easily apparent whether one reply or individual replies is more appropriate.

If you've received several emails from one person and, given how long some of the earlier emails have been waiting in your inbox, you can identify that all of the emails can easily be addressed with one compilation reply, write and send the reply email now and then move the whole batch of emails into your actioned emails folder. Although it may take a couple of minutes of your time, it will be deliciously rewarding to see a whole bunch of emails leave your inbox forever.

On the other hand, if you feel that you would still need to address each email individually, or if the reply requires some additional work on your part, leave the emails right where they are for now. Remember that, at this stage, we are more interested in doing a quick purge of the emails that can easily and permanently leave your inbox.

Another benefit of sorting your emails by the From field when clearing out your email backlog is that it will allow you to easily delete unnecessary emails in one go. In Outlook, you can click on the sender's name (directly above the first email from that sender) to automatically select all of the emails from that person. You can then hit the Delete key and watch them disappear. Of course, make sure it is appropriate to delete all of the emails – this will usually only be the case for newsletters and other impersonal notifications, such as a daily deals newsletter, catalogues from stores, daily omnibuses of social media notifications, and updates from crowdfunding websites.

Your task is now very much underway, and it is simply a matter of you continuing with this process for every sender from A to Z.

When working through your email backlog, you will need to make a decision about each email that you come across, and the options you have available are as follows:

1. Delete the email: if it is spam, or no longer applies given how long it has been since it was first received, and you believe you will never need it again.
2. Move the email into your Actioned Emails folder: if you have previously replied to the email, or if the email is so old that it no longer requires a reply but you still feel you should keep a copy of the email anyway, or if it contained important information, such as a work-related newsletter.
3. Reply to the email: if the reply can be written and sent *within two minutes*, do it now and then store the original in your Actioned Emails folder and move on.
4. Leave the email in your inbox: if the email requires further action on your part or would take a significant amount of time to action.

Important note: don't get used to the idea of number four above: putting an email in the proverbial Too Hard basket and leaving it for later. This is the *only* time you are allowed to take such an action.

We're in damage control mode here, working through an overwhelming email backlog and wrangling at into something that will be more manageable for you in the coming days. Once you've mastered your overflowing inbox and achieved Zero Inbox for the first time, you will move into daily maintenance mode and you will no longer have the option to leave an email in your inbox to deal with "later." After all, that's what got you in this mess in the first place.

The process of working through your email backlog will take as long as it takes. It is an additional task that you need to find time for in amongst your regular daily tasks, and you may find that it can take a week or more for you to dump all of your various inbox storage folders into your one main inbox, quickly review every email and make a decision based on the four options listed above.

Don't worry how long the process takes: just keep in mind that this is something you're only ever going to have two deal with once. Any progress is progress nonetheless, and know that you will get there eventually.

Step 3 – Set Yourself Up For Success

By this stage you've worked through your entire email backlog: well done! That was no easy task, and although it may have taken you days or even weeks to achieve, you got there in the end.

The hard work isn't quite over yet, though, as you still have emails in your inbox that you've been saving for a significant amount of time, and you now know that the emails still in your inbox are those that still need to be replied to or otherwise actioned.

But, although you're still somewhat in the email backlog stage, you've now also progressed the ongoing maintenance stage. This is where you need to know how to set yourself up for success so that you never find yourself with a cluttered, unmanageable inbox ever again. You also need to learn how to deal with emails on a daily basis in an efficient and effective way: but we'll get to that in the next step. For now, let's examine the things you need to do to set yourself up for future success.

Turn Off Notifications

Turn off any notifications that alert you when a new email is received. On some level, you probably already recognise just how much of a distraction and an interruption those almost-constant dings and pings are, and the effect that they have on your productivity.

Although we are aiming to conquer your emails and achieve Zero Inbox every day, we are *not* going to do that by spending all day in your inbox. Emails need to be scheduled just as you would schedule your lunch break, a phone call, or a meeting, and you shouldn't be dipping into your inbox constantly. Disabling new email alerts and other email notifications will go a long way towards removing the temptation to continually check your emails.

You may argue that your particular job circumstances dictate that you check your emails at all times, and that may be the case. Perhaps you need to be on-call if your boss sends you an email, or perhaps your job depends on you replying to specific customer service emails promptly. If that is true for you, you can set up special rules within your email program that will alert you to certain types of emails only, within parameters that you will set up in advance.

For example, you could set up an alert that would notify you every time your manager sends you an email, or an alert that notifies you when a specific type of customer service email arrives. Play with the settings until you are satisfied that you will properly be notified of any emails that genuinely do require your immediate attention. That doesn't change the fact, though, you do not need to be notified when you receive a personal email from a friend, when you receive an email from Amazon with the latest Kindle releases.

Unsubscribe As You Go

I previously advised you to not worry about unsubscribing from unwanted emails while working through your email backlog. Dealing with hundreds or thousands of long forgotten emails is a hard enough task on its own, so that wasn't the time to worry about unsubscribing.

But now that you have dealt with the bulk of your email inbox, you need to be vigilant about what you remain subscribed to. If you find that you delete an email from a particular sender automatically, that is a sure sign that you should unsubscribe yourself from the mailing list altogether. Social media alerts are a prime target for unsubscribing. And just because it seemed like a good idea to sign up for a Recipe a Day mailing list, doesn't mean that the ongoing newsletters are still serving you today. It is usually (and should be, according to laws in most countries) a simple matter of clicking the *unsubscribe* button at the bottom of the email and then following the prompts on the website that opens afterwards.

Worst case scenario, you find that you miss your daily recipe and wish that you still received at: just subscribe again. You're not burning any bridges by unsubscribing and removing yourself from someone else's mailing list, as they'll surely be happy to have you back as a subscriber later.

From experience, though, it is highly unlikely that will ever miss any of the ongoing updates and newsletters that you've been regularly receiving until now. If you're really feeling anxious about it, make a list of everything that you unsubscribe from so that you'll know where to find it again if you change your mind.

Keep in mind that the aim of this step is to unsubscribe from anything that you automatically delete or do little more than skim read every time you receive it. There may be some mailing lists that you are very happy to stay subscribed to. Personally, I look forward to receiving updates from College Humour, and I allow myself the guilty pleasure of opening up a few of the links in their daily email to see the latest jokes and comics they've created. It's something that I look forward to every day and I don't deny myself the pleasure, since there are very few other ways that I allow myself to procrastinate while working. Identify one or two mailing lists that you are happy to stay a part of, and allow yourself the privilege of continuing. The cost is, of course, you must unsubscribe from anything else that takes up valuable space in your inbox and that you're only going to swiftly delete anyway.

The One Thing You'll Need - The 10 Minute Timer

I claimed in the introduction that I'm not selling anything: no course, no dreaded coaching plans, and no software, and that there is nothing you would need to purchase in order to follow all the steps in this book, take control of your overflowing inbox, and achieve Zero Inbox every day.

While that remains true, there is one caveat I should make: there is one thing you'll need in order to put these steps to practice for you. But it's something that most people will already have, and everyone else will be able to get for free, so I didn't really lie. I did say that there's nothing you need to *buy*, but there *is* one thing you'll need.

You know that I'm not an advocate of buying programs, tools, or apps to help you with your inbox. The idea behind this book is that you need nothing to achieve Zero Inbox every day except a set of rules that you stick to without fail.

My exception to this is a simple 10-minute timer. Most smartphones (and even some old-school talk-n-text phones) have a timer or alarm app included, or you can download one for free. A simple search in the Google Play Store or the App Store should find plenty of suitable and free apps. It doesn't matter which one you choose as long as it's free and allows you to set a simple 10-minute countdown timer (not counting up like a stopwatch).

If you're really looking to simplify, a regular kitchen timer or egg timer will work just fine.

I'll discuss the purpose of the 10-minute timer in a later chapter, but for now just make sure that you have access to something – anything – that will accurately count down 10 minutes and make a sound when it's done.

Step 4 – Learn The Art of Short Emails

Be a Leader with Short Emails

Achieving Zero Inbox each day takes as long as it takes. As you know by now, you need to completely action every email, no matter what that involves, before archiving it. Sometimes that will take half a second for you to click Delete, and other times actioning one email will take a considerable chunk of your day.

Unfortunately, that's just the way it is: just like how some people in your life require more "upkeep" than other people, some emails are more demanding of your time and energy than other emails.

But there is a way to spend less time on each email, and in some cases to save yourself an hour or more.

Write short emails.

Not just shorter, but *short*. A few sentences, at max. There aren't many situations that call for novel-length emails. In fact, I would argue that there are *no* legitimate circumstances that call for emails longer than a paragraph or two. Anything longer than that should probably be contained in an attachment rather than the body of an email.

You know who writes short emails?

People who are extremely busy. People who don't have the time to write out a long reply. People who have carved out about 15 seconds of their valuable time to respond to an email. People who you can almost guarantee will never think of that email again after they have sent their response.

And you know who writes long emails?

People with nothing better to do. People who are emotionally invested in the subject matter of the email, or exceptionally interested in the person they're sending it to. A long email is a dead giveaway that the sender is extremely interested in the subject of the email or the person they're sending it to, or both. Look out for those people who continue to send you long emails and you'll start to notice a pattern.

In your business life in particular, which of those people do you want to be?

Here's a bonus book within this book. It's called "How to Appear Busy and Important."

And here's the text of the book.

"Write short emails."

Somehow, I don't think I'd sell many copies of a book with a six-word title and three words of content, but it remains true nonetheless.

Writing short emails makes you look busy and important.

Busy and important people don't have time to write long emails. Busy and important people got that way because they know how to get stuff done.

There are plenty of other benefits of writing short emails.

Not everyone knows what you now know about emails and so not everyone knows that emails need to be tackled in chronological order and as soon as possible. If you send someone a long email, there is a very good chance that they will put your email into some kind of crazy "reply later" folder, or will just leave it to rot with the other long-forgotten emails in their inbox. Writing a long email often means your email is going to send a fair amount of time in the recipient's inbox and you won't get a reply as quickly as you may have liked.

Writing short emails is a skill. In fact, writing short *anything* is a skill. Keep your emails short, and people will come to recognise the skill that that has taken. David Belasco, an American theatrical producer who lived in the late 1800s and early 1900s purportedly said: "If you can't write your idea on the back of my calling card, you don't have a clear idea."

More so than ever today, people value clarity and brevity. People are reading their emails on their mobile devices while waiting at traffic lights or on public transport, and they don't want to be scrolling down page after page while you ramble on. Before you click "Send," picture your recipient reading your email on their smart watch while in the bathroom. Did you get your point across in a few lines, or are they furrowing their brow and squinting while they scroll down line after line?

How to Write Short Emails

Firstly, a short email is not a rude one. A short email can – must – still contain all of the niceties expected in today's society.

Stop rambling. Think before writing. Pretend you're back in the good ol' days when correspondence was either hand-written or typed on a typewriter. Yes, pen can be crossed out and typewriter ink can be erased, but not without making the whole document look messy and unprofessional.

For a flawless finish, people needed to get things right the first time, which meant they needed to think about what they were going to say before they put it on paper, otherwise they'd have to start all over again.

Take that same approach today with your emails. Before diving in to a long, rambling response, simply stop for a moment, take a sip of your coffee or water if you feel the need to keep moving, and consider what you want to say. Then say it in the least number of words possible.

The trick is to go through the thought process *before* you start writing. Work out what you want to say, think about how you'll say it, and then start composing your reply. Once you start thinking about your reply first, you'll realise just how often in the past you've dived straight into a reply without first knowing what you intend to say.

Why do we do this?

Because sometimes we're asked a question that we don't know how to answer, so diving straight in with a rambling reply that doesn't actually address the question at hand is just another way of procrastinating. It makes you feel as if you're being productive when in actuality you're just boring everyone with a reply that manages to skirt the real issue. Work out the answer to the question or the message you want to get across *before* you start.

Be direct. Sometimes the need for niceties get in the way of actually enunciating what you want.

Here's a particularly nauseating example:

If you don't mind, when you've got a moment, would you please review the attached report and let me know what you think? I'd really appreciate any help or advice you could give.

Argh! That is frustrating to write and even worse to receive.

Instead, try:

Please review the attached report and send your feedback. Thanks!

You've still included both a please and a thankyou, so your need for politeness and good manners are met while still being direct and succinct. In my opinion, the exclamation point on the "Thanks!" lightens the tone so that it doesn't appear snappy or forceful.

One Topic per Email

Always, always stick to one topic per email. Discussing multiple topics in one email leads to confusion and delays as the recipient will not reply until they can answer every part of your email. If you ask five questions in one email, you'll have to wait until the recipient can confidently answer all five questions – and until they feel they have the time and headspace to tackle your long list of questions – before you get a reply.

This also allows you to make excellent use of your subject line. Many people throw away the subject line by leaving it blank or writing something generic like "Hi!". The subject line is valuable real estate in the recipient's inbox. It, along with the sender's name and the date and time is the only information they'll have before opening the email, and it will form the basis of their decision whether to open your email or not. The subject line is therefore the only variable that you can manipulate and the only input you have to inform their decision about your email immediately after receiving it. With only one topic per email, go right ahead and put the topic in the subject line of the email.

Yes, it sounds tedious, but create one new email for every topic. Your emails will be short and to the point, and the recipient will be able to answer each topic completely. In addition, the recipient will be able to immediately answer the emails containing the question that they do know the answers to, and can hold off on the more complicated questions.

Say you send a colleague an email with five questions: four simple ones, and one complicated question that the recipient doesn't immediately know the answer to. If you put all five questions in one email, you'll probably have to wait until the recipient can answer the one difficult question before getting a reply to *any* of them. Alternatively, you may get a reply with the answers to the four easy questions and a promise of a further reply with the answer to the fifth question, which may never come since your email has already been marked as having been replied to.

On the other hand, if you sent five separate emails each containing one question, the recipient will be able to shoot back answers to the simple questions, and will be reminded that they still need to answer the fifth question because that particular email will not yet have been replied to.

Yes, you may feel silly creating five emails all at once. But you will be glad later when you can track the entire conversation relating to each distinct topic in one email thread. And you can bet that the recipient will be grateful for your organisation and foresight.

Make Good Use of Templates

Depending on your job and the reasons that you use email, you may find that you send variations of the same message several times. Perhaps you work in customer service and you find that you answer the same questions over and again. Perhaps you are due to have a baby and your family, friends, and co-workers keep emailing you, asking for an update. Whatever the situation, if you find yourself writing the same content over and over, it may be time to use a template.

You know by now that I am a big fan of simplifying matters as much as possible. Most email clients will allow you to create a template that you can customise and send off with a few clicks of the mouse. And if this is something that you'd like to explore, a simple Google search or a play around in your email client will show you how to set up templates that will work for you.

On the other hand, I prefer to keep things as simple as possible, so I use a good old-fashioned Notepad document to create, store, and access my templates. Anytime I find that I'm writing the same response over and again, I'll add the text of the email to my template document. Anything that needs to be personalised, such as the name of the recipient, the date, or anything else, I replace with a series of upper case Xs – enough of them so that my eyes are immediately drawn to each instance so that I don't accidentally send off the email without properly personalising it.

The reason that I am drawn towards DIY email templates a low-tech solution such as a Notepad document is because I'm concerned that a pre-made template created within an email client, such as Outlook or Gmail, may be sent out without being properly customised. What if someone was complaining about late delivery of an order, and I use a premade template that I forgot included a link to a feedback form and a request that they leave public feedback? The last thing I want is for an unhappy customer to leave feedback before I had the chance to resolve the problem and turn them back into a happy customer.

I prefer pasting in my own template sections on a case-by-case basis, while still composing the email reply in the same way that I would any other email, so that I always maintain strict control over the contents of the email. But if you feel happy to try turning one of your prewritten messages into a template within your email client, by all means please do so.

Step 5 – Knowing When To Quit

If the topic of an email conversation is starting to get long and complicated; if things are beginning to get heated or a disagreement is brewing; or if you don't think you can adequately answer the email in a succinct way: there is just one way forward.

Pick up the phone.

Sometimes email just isn't the right medium for a particular conversation. Sometimes what starts out as a simple exchange boils over into something more emotional or complicated. A simple rule is that if there are emotions involved, pick up the phone. Tone does not carry well over email, and it is easy to misinterpret what is being said (no matter how many emojis you use).

Pick up the phone.

If you can't get through, or if the recipient is in a different time zone, then immediately create an appointment in your calendar for the next possible time for you to make the call (within the next 12 hours if possible) and attach the email to your appointment. You can then properly treat the original email as having been actioned, since you've done everything you can do with this email for the time being, and you have moved it to your calendar to be followed up at a specific time and date in the very near future.

For bonus points, send a quick reply along the lines of "I will phone you to discuss at [time]." Don't get bogged down in the topic of the email if you're going to phone them anyway. In other words, don't go anywhere near something like this:

"I don't agree with you, and I've got 17 good reasons why. I'll go through all of them in excruciating detail over the phone."

Guess whose number will be stored as "Do Not Answer"? No, if you're going to call, do it now. If you can't get through or if it's 2 a.m. in their time zone, schedule the phone call in your calendar and, optionally, tell them that you'll call at the appropriate time. Leave the substance for the call. When you get the reminder, open the email from within your calendar and refer to it during your call.

If you use a physical wall calendar or planner, still schedule the call as before but print out a copy of the email and staple it to your wall calendar or put it in your planner on the correct day. This will save you time since you won't have to go searching for the email later. It will also make you look more efficient if the person calls you in the meantime and you've got the information to hand.

Step 6 – Actioning Every Email

You've worked through your backlog: congratulations! That was no easy task, but hopefully you've been rewarded for your hard work by the feeling of freedom and clarity that comes with a clear, tidy inbox.

Now you're at the stage where you can aim to achieve Zero Inbox every day. And this is where the rules change a little from those that you followed when working through your email backlog.

Firstly, you will no longer your emails by the From field. From now on, emails by the Date field, and will always action emails in strict chronological order. You'll tackle emails in the order in which they arrive, while resisting the temptation to skip ahead or leave an email for later.

Why Your Inbox Is Not For Storage

There is never a good reason to store an email in your inbox. I'm sure your brain is busy thinking up exceptions to this rule, but let me stop you there – there aren't any. There is never a good reason to store an email in your inbox, and that is because there is always something you can do to action that email right now.

Here is a probably-not-exhaustive list of the possible actions you can take with any email in your inbox.

Emails That Ask For Something: Hot Potato It Right Back

If you have all the information that you need, reply to the email immediately and then move the original email into your archive folder. I call it the Hot Potato because the aim is to get the email out of your hands and back into theirs as soon as possible.

Schedule the Appointment

If the email contains details of an upcoming event or appointment, reply to the email to confirm (if necessary, though this will not be necessary for a computer-generated appointment confirmation notice).

Then open up your calendar and immediately enter the details of the appointment in your calendar. Once you have the appointment created, attach the original email to your appointment. In Outlook, this is as simple as physically dragging the email from your inbox and dropping it into the large white text area in your appointment.

If you still use a physical calendar, the process is much the same. Write the details of the appointment or event on your calendar, then print out the original email. Staple the email to your calendar.

The idea of keeping the email with your calendar is so that you will have all the information that you need when it comes time to attending your appointment. You have the address on hand, along with the original appointment time if, like me, you feel the need to check it ten times before you attend, as well as the contact details of the organiser in case you need to contact them beforehand. Once these steps have been taken, archive the original email.

How to Handle Forwarded Jokes, Articles, Videos

If the email contains a link to an article that may be of interest, or a link to a funny video or any other kind of link that is purely for entertainment purposes, now is *not* the time to be opening that link. Create a document on your computer (or ideally in a shared folder that you can access from all your devices such as Dropbox or Google Drive) to store these links for later viewing. I prefer to use an Excel spreadsheet and to have two separate tabs: one for things to read, and the other for things to watch or listen to.

Note that you are not saving the email for later, just the *link* to the thing that you're going to read, view or listen to. You are still going to action the email straight away. Hit reply and thank the person for sending whatever it is to you. Tell them that you're at work and don't have time to read it/watch it/listen to it right now, but that you plan to do so on your lunch break/tonight/over the weekend.
Then store the email, because you have done everything that you need to do with it. Later, while you're having your lunch or a coffee break or even just taking a moment to procrastinate from work, you've got a list of funny and interesting things ready for you to read.

You may be thinking: *Why can't I just leave the email in my inbox, and watch the video or read the article on my lunch break and reply to the email then?*

No way. There is a huge difference between leaving an email sitting in your inbox, and the method that I have described. In my method, you are actioning the email immediately, just as you are supposed to do. The fact that the link contained in the email is not urgent or work-related means that it is fine to save the *content* for later, but you must still deal with the *email* itself right now. If, after watching the video or reading the article, you have a further comment to make to the person who sent it to you originally, by all means open up a new email at that time. But this will be a new conversation, not the continuation of the original email.

Most of the time you'll be free to enjoy the content without following up. And of course, if the same person has sent you several entertainment-related emails in a row, you can just send one short blanket reply thanking them for providing you with some valuable procrastination material ready for when you need it the most.

Dealing with Personal Emails

If the email is a personal one from a friend or family member, or even from a colleague but of an entirely personal nature (not work-related at all), you still need to reply to that email right now.

Here is where your 10-minute timer comes into play. Set a 10-minute timer (on your computer, phone or even a physical timer like a kitchen timer or the timer on your microwave) and give yourself exactly 10 minutes to reply to that email. This will force you to keep it brief, but will still give you enough time to properly answer any questions that were asked in the email, and to comment on any news that was raised.

If someone has taken the time to write a personal email to you, this is similar to someone sending you a letter in the mail in days gone by, and it deserves a response. It does not, however, warrant you spending all day on it to the exclusion of your actual work, but by the same token it does not deserve to sit around in your inbox for two weeks until you get around to replying.

Reply immediately, but when that 10-minute timer goes off, you sign off – mid paragraph if you have to. People are used to having emails abruptly end with something like: *Better get back to work!* so don't think that you are rude for signing off. What is rude is what most people do: choose to not reply for weeks simply because the email is hidden amongst thousands of other emails in their overflowing inboxes.
Old habits die hard, and there are times when I too would love nothing more than to file an email away for later. There are usually two types of emails that I instantly want to throw in the virtual too-hard basket: client emails that are complicated or annoying; and personal emails.

Surely there's nothing more annoying than when you're almost at the end of your working day, you're powering through your inbox, only a few emails to go, Zero Inbox in sight, and you come down to a three-page email from your aunt with all the news from home. Or a long-winded essay from your old high school friend detailing her children's latest antics.

Surely *these* emails can be filed away for later, right? You'll tackle them on the weekend, or some other time when you've got time to write a long response, to answer every question and comment on every paragraph.

Wrong. Personal emails may make you sigh but they are not an exception to the roles of Zero Inbox. They must be tackled in the first instance and completely actioned – in this case, replied to – before being archived.

But there is a trick that will help, and that is to limit the amount of time you spend on your reply.

Foregoing Niceties

Make an agreement with your closest family and friends to forgo all niceties in all future emails. This sounds strange, I know, but I can guarantee it will be a relief for both of you. Sometimes you just want to send a link to an interesting article or a funny video, but you don't because you know you'll need to construct a polite email around it. How many times have you written an email like this?

Dear [Friend's Name],
Hey, how are you? How's work going? I hope you're having a great week so far.
I saw this today and couldn't help but think of you.
http://theoatmeal.com/comics/printers
Printers, huh? How frustrating.
Anyway, I'd better get back to work. Do you have anything interesting planned for the weekend so far?
Take care, talk to you later.

Ugh. That took way too much time and effort and it still came out stilted and awkward. It is not how you would speak in real life and it's completely unnecessary.

Yes, you may need to write emails like this to your colleagues, superiors, and clients, but presumably you wouldn't be sending them a funny online comic either. So for your close friends and family members, make an agreement to forgo all niceties, including opening greetings and closing greetings. Explain to them why, and that your sole purpose is not to be rude but to open up email communication so that you are both free to email each other as much and as often as you like without being bogged down by formalities.

You're way more likely to actually send that interesting article or funny Internet thing to someone if you don't have to spend 10 minutes thinking of every polite question you need to ask them.
Choose one person now, call them up on the phone and have a two-minute conversation with them about this idea. Get them on board, try it for a week, and then see how you're feeling about it. I can guarantee that in one week's time you will be calling up a host of other family members and friends and making the same deal.

Then you be sending emails like this:

http://theoatmeal.com/comics/printers
Printers, huh?

They'll be glad to receive them, and you'll be getting similar ones from them. No reply is necessary, but if they did have something they wanted to say regarding the article, joke, photo, or whatever you've sent, they can safely reply in one sentence, again forgoing the niceties.

It's liberating. And the sooner more people get on board, the freer everyone will be.

Step 7 – Moving Forward

You have made tremendous progress by following the steps set out in this book. By now, you have set up an effective and simple storage system within your email client (nothing could be simpler than one folder to store all your actioned and sent emails), you've worked through the backlog of emails, and arrived at a point where you can effectively manage your inbox on a daily basis.

You've learned how to write short emails and why it's important that you do so, how to forgo niceties when emailing family and friends, and how to deal with forwarded jokes, articles, and videos.

You have all the skills that you need in order to achieve Zero Inbox every day. How long will this take each day? This will inevitably vary depending on the emails you receive each day. We all know the one email can take an hour or more to reply to, especially if it involves gathering information or filling in forms. But what's important is that, regardless of the amount or content of emails you receive on any given day, you stick with the plan of action in each email in turn, in chronological order.

Yes, your ten minute reply to Aunt Judy may have to wait for an hour while you compile financial information and email completed forms back to your bank manager, but that's infinitely better than the old system, where Aunt Judy's email was lost among hundreds of spammy newsletters, work emails, forwarded videos, and other email clutter.

One final word of warning: do not be tempted to change the rules and prioritise your emails. Although it may sound sensible to instigate a rule that work emails should be replied to before skim-reading and deleting shopping newsletters or writing a ten-minute reply to a personal email, this will be a slippery slope to disaster.

The point is that most emails do not take long to action. Tackling emails in strict chronological order may mean that a work email will have to wait for 15 minutes as you schedule an appointment, unsubscribe from an annoying newsletter, and send a quick reply to a personal email, but in the end it still only 15 minutes. You could easily have spent that time on the phone or procrastinating by flicking through your Facebook feed. If you start being selective about which emails you reply to now and which you leave for later, you will very quickly end up with a cluttered inbox that looks a lot like the one you had before you started reading this book.
It may seem counterintuitive to browse through a clothes catalogue email before answering a work email, but if that's the order that the emails arrived in, it's the order in which they should be tackled.

Any deviations from strict chronological order will very quickly lead you back to the mess you started from. The trick is to keep your replies short, unsubscribe from newsletters and mailing lists that no longer serve you, and keep working through your inbox in chronological order.

Then just sit back and smile when other people brag about the thousands of emails in their inboxes, knowing that they still think that a cluttered inbox, full of emails that should have been replied to weeks ago, is a sign of success. Because now you know better.